S

CW00828333

"He that heareth you, heareth me; and he that despiseth you, despiseth me; and he that despiseth me, despiseth him that sent me." —Luke 10:16

SCRIPTURE ALONE?

21 REASONS TO REJECT "SOLA SCRIPTURA"

By

Joel S. Peters

"Therefore, brethren, stand fast; and hold the traditions which you have learned, whether by word, or by our epistle." —2 Thessalonians 2:14

TAN BOOKS AND PUBLISHERS, INC.
Rockford, Illinois 61105

Nihil Obstat:

    David D. Kagan, J.C.L.
    Vicar General

Imprimatur:

   ✠ Thomas G. Doran, D.D., J.C.D.
    Bishop of Rockford
    Rockford, Illinois
    August 6, 2001

The Nihil Obstat and Imprimatur are official declarations that a book or pamphlet is free of doctrinal or moral error. No implication is contained therein that those who have granted the Nihil Obstat and Imprimatur agree with the contents, opinions or statements expressed.

ISBN 0-89555-640-5

Library of Congress Catalog Card No.: 98-61405

Printed and bound in the United States of America.

TAN BOOKS AND PUBLISHERS, INC.
P.O. Box 424
Rockford, Illinois 61105
1999

"I would not believe the Gospel itself, if the authority of the Catholic Church did not move me to do so."

—St. Augustine (354-430)
(*Contra Epist. Fundam.* i, 6)

About the Author

Joel Peters currently teaches theology at St. Joseph Regional High School in Montvale, New Jersey. He obtained his B.A. in Psychology/Sociology from Rutgers University and his M.A. in Pastoral Ministry from Immaculate Conception Seminary at Seton Hall University. Over the years, Mr. Peters has been involved in many forms of parish ministry and youth ministry. His personal interests include apologetics, the study of cults, and the Shroud of Turin. Joel Peters' articles have appeared in *This Rock* magazine. He is married and is the father of three children.

CONTENTS

viii *Scripture Alone?*

SCRIPTURE ALONE?

What Is *Sola Scriptura*?

"We believe in the Bible alone and the Bible in its entirety as the sole rule of faith for the Christian!"

You may have heard these words or something very similar to them from a Fundamentalist or Evangelical Protestant. They are, in essence, the meaning of the doctrine of *Sola Scriptura*, or "Scripture alone," which alleges that the Bible—as interpreted by the individual believer—is the only source of religious authority and is the Christian's sole *rule of faith* or criterion regarding what is to be believed. By this doctrine, which is one of the foundational beliefs of Protestantism, a Protestant denies that there is any other source of religious authority or divine Revelation to humanity.

The Catholic, on the other hand, holds that the immediate or direct *rule of faith* is the teaching of the Church; the Church in turn takes her teaching from divine Revelation—both the *written Word*, called Sacred Scripture, and the oral or *unwritten Word*, known as "Tradition." The teaching authority or "Magisterium" of the Catholic

Church (headed by the Pope), although not itself a source of divine Revelation, nevertheless has a God-given mission to interpret and teach both Scripture and Tradition. Scripture and Tradition are the *sources* of Christian doctrine, the Christian's remote or indirect *rule of faith.*

Obviously these two views on what constitutes the Christian's *rule of faith* are opposed to each other, and anyone who sincerely seeks to follow Christ must be sure that he follows the one that is true.

The doctrine of *Sola Scriptura* originated with Martin Luther, the 16th-century German monk who broke away from the Roman Catholic Church and started the Protestant "Reformation."[1] In response to some abuses that had been occurring within the Catholic Church, Luther became a vocal opponent of certain practices. As far as these abuses were concerned, they were real and Luther was justified in reacting. However, as a series of confrontations between him and the Catholic hierarchy developed, the issues became more centered on the question of Church authority and—from Luther's perspective—whether or not the teaching of the Catholic Church was a legitimate *rule of faith* for Christians.

As the confrontations between Luther and the Church's hierarchy ensued and tensions mounted, Luther accused the Catholic Church of having corrupted Christian doctrine and having distorted

Biblical truths, and he more and more came to believe that the Bible, as interpreted by the individual believer, was the only true religious authority for a Christian. He eventually rejected Tradition as well as the teaching authority of the Catholic Church (with the Pope at its head) as having legitimate religious authority.

An honest inquirer must ask, then, whether Luther's doctrine of "Scripture alone" was a genuine restoration of a Biblical truth or rather the promulgation of an individual's personal views on Christian authority. Luther was clearly passionate about his beliefs, and he was successful in spreading them, but these facts in and of themselves do not guarantee that what he taught was correct. Since one's spiritual well-being, and even one's eternal destiny, is at stake, the Christian believer needs to be absolutely sure in this matter.

Following are twenty-one considerations which will help the reader scrutinize Luther's doctrine of *Sola Scriptura* from Biblical, historical and logical bases and which show that it is not in fact a genuine Biblical truth, but rather a man-made doctrine.

1. The Doctrine of *Sola Scriptura* Is Not Taught Anywhere in the Bible.

Perhaps the most striking reason for rejecting this doctrine is that there is not one verse anywhere in the Bible in which it is taught, and it therefore becomes a self-refuting doctrine.

Protestants often point to verses such as *2 Timothy* 3:16-17 or *The Apocalypse* (*Revelation*) 22:18-19 in defense of *Sola Scriptura*, but close examination of these two passages easily demonstrates that they do not support the doctrine at all.

In *2 Timothy* 3:16-17 we read, "All scripture, inspired of God, is profitable to teach, to reprove, to correct, to instruct in justice, that the man of God may be perfect, furnished to every good work." There are five considerations which undermine the *Sola Scriptura* interpretation of this passage:

1) The Greek word *ophelimos* ("profitable") used in verse 16 means "useful" and not "sufficient." An example of this difference would be to say that water is useful for our existence—even necessary—but it is not sufficient; that is, it is not the only thing we need to survive. We also need food, clothing, shelter, etc. Likewise, Scripture is useful in the life of the believer, but it was never meant to be the only source of Christian teaching, the only thing needed for believers.

2) The Greek word *pasa*, which is often rendered as "all," actually means "every," and it has the sense of referring to each and every one of the class denoted by the noun connected with it.[2] In other words, the Greek reads in a way which indicates that each and every "Scripture" is profitable.

If the doctrine of *Sola Scriptura* were true, then based on the Greek in verse 16, each and every book of the Bible could stand on its own as the sole rule of faith, a position which is obviously absurd.

3) The "Scripture" that St. Paul is referring to here is the Old Testament, a fact which is made plain by his reference to the Scriptures' being known by Timothy from "infancy" (verse 15). The New Testament as we know it did not yet exist, or at best it was incomplete, so it simply could not have been included in St. Paul's understanding of what was meant by the term "scripture." If we take St. Paul's words at face value, *Sola Scriptura* would therefore mean that the Old Testament is the Christian's sole rule of faith. This is a premise that all Christians would reject.

Protestants may respond to this issue by arguing that St. Paul is not here discussing the *canon* of the Bible (the authoritative list of which books are included in the Bible), but rather the *nature* of Scripture. While there is some validity to this assertion, the issue of canon *is* also relevant here, for the following reason: Before we can talk about the nature of Scripture as being *theopneustos* or "inspired" (literally, "God-breathed"), it is imperative that we identify with certainty those books we mean when we say "Scripture"; otherwise, the wrong writings may be labeled as "inspired." St. Paul's words here obviously took on a new dimension when the New Testament was completed, as Christians eventually considered it, too, to be "Scripture." It can be argued, then, that the Biblical canon *is* also the issue here, as St. Paul—writing under the inspiration of the Holy Spirit—emphasizes the fact that *all* (and not just *some*) Scripture is inspired. The question that begs to be asked, however, is this: "How can we be sure we have *all* the correct writings?" Obviously, we can only know the answer if we know what the canon of the Bible is. Such a question poses a problem for the Protestant, but not for the Catholic, as the latter has an infallible authority to answer it.

4) The Greek word *artios*, here translated "perfect," may at first glance make it seem that the Scriptures are indeed all that is needed. "After all," one may ask, "if the Scriptures make the man of God perfect, what else could be needed? Doesn't the very word 'perfect' imply that nothing is lacking?"

Well, the difficulty with such an interpretation is that the text here does not say that it is *solely* by means of the Scriptures that the man of God is made "perfect." The text—if anything—indicates precisely the opposite to be true, namely, that the Scriptures operate in conjunction with other things. Notice that it is not just anyone who is made perfect, but rather the "man of God"—which means a minister of Christ (cf. *1 Tim.* 6:11), a clergyman. The fact that this individual is a minister of Christ presupposes that he has already had training and teaching which prepared him to assume his office. This being the case, the Scriptures would be merely one item in a series of items which make this man of God "perfect." The Scriptures may complete his list of necessary items or they may be one prominent item on the list, but surely they are not the *only* item on his list nor intended to be *all* that he needs.

By way of analogy, consider a medical doctor. In this context we might say something like, "The *Physician's Desk Reference* [a standard medical reference book] makes our General Practitioner perfect, so that he may be ready to treat any medical situation." Obviously such a statement does not mean that all a doctor needs is his *PDR*. It is either the last item on his list or just one prominent item. The doctor also needs his stethoscope, his blood pressure gauge, his training, etc. These other items are presupposed by the fact that we are talking about a doctor rather than a non-medical person. So it would be incorrect to assume that if the *PDR* makes the doctor "perfect," it is the *only* thing which makes him so.

Also, taking this word "perfect" as meaning "the only necessary item" results in a biblical contradiction, for in *James* 1:4 we read that patience—rather than the Scriptures—makes one perfect: "And patience hath a perfect work; that you may be perfect and entire, failing in nothing."

Now it is true that a different Greek word (*teleios*) is used here for "perfect," but the fact remains that the basic meaning is the same. Now, if one rightly acknowledges that patience is clearly not the only thing a Christian needs in order to be perfect, then a consistent interpretive method would compel one to acknowledge likewise that the Scriptures are not the *only* thing a "man of God" needs in order to be perfect.

5) The Greek word *exartizo* in verse 17, here translated "furnished" (other Bible versions read something like "fully equipped" or "thoroughly furnished") is referred to by Protestants as "proof" of *Sola Scriptura,* since this word—again—may be taken as implying that nothing else is needed for the "man of God." However, even though the man of God may be "furnished" or "thoroughly equipped," this fact in and of itself does not guarantee that he knows how to interpret correctly and apply any given Scripture passage. The clergyman must also be taught how to correctly *use* the Scriptures, even though he may already be "furnished" with them.

Consider again a medical analogy. Picture a medical student at the beginning of an internship. He might have at his disposal all the equipment necessary to perform an operation (i.e., he is "thoroughly equipped" or "furnished" for a surgical procedure), but until he spends time with the doctors, who are the resident authorities, observing their techniques, learning their skills, and practicing some procedures of his own, the surgical instruments at his disposal are essentially useless. In fact, if he does not learn how to use these instruments *properly*, they can actually become dangerous in his hands.

So it is with the "man of God" and the Scriptures. The Scriptures, like the surgical instruments, are life-giving only when properly used. When improperly used, the exact opposite results can occur. In one case they could bring physical ruin or even death; in the other case they could bring spiritual ruin or even spiritual death. Since the Bible admonishes us to *handle rightly* or *rightly divide* the word of truth (cf. *2 Tim.* 2:15), it is therefore possible to *handle incorrectly* or *wrongly divide* it—much like an untrained medical student who incorrectly wields his surgical instruments.

Regarding *The Apocalypse (Revelation)* 22:18-19, there are two considerations which undermine the *Sola Scriptura* interpretation of these verses. The passage—almost the very last in the Bible—reads: "For I testify to every one that heareth the words of the prophecy of this book: If any man shall add to these things, God shall add unto him the plagues written in this book. And if any man shall take away from the words of the book of this prophecy, God shall take away his part out of the book of life, and out of the holy city, and from these things that are written in this book."

1) When these verses say that nothing is to be added to or taken from the "words of the prophecy of this book," they are not referring to Sacred Tradition being "added" to Sacred Scripture. It is obvious from the context that the "book" being referred to here is *Revelation* or *The Apocalypse* and not the whole Bible. We know this because St. John says that anyone who is guilty of adding to "this book" will be cursed with the plagues "written in this book," namely the plagues *he* described earlier *in his own book, Revelation*. To assert otherwise is to do violence to the text and to distort its plain meaning, especially since the Bible as we know it did not exist when this passage was written and therefore could not be what was meant.[3]

In defense of their interpretation of these verses, Protestants will often contend that God knew in advance what the canon of Scripture would be, with *Revelation* being the last book of the Bible, and thus He "sealed" that canon with the words of verses 18-19. But this interpretation involves reading a meaning into the text. Furthermore, if such an assertion were true, how is it that the Christian knows unmistakably that *Revelation* 22:18-19 is "sealing" the canon unless an infallible teaching authority assures him that this is the correct interpretation of that verse? But if such an infallible authority exists, then the *Sola Scriptura* doctrine becomes *ipso facto* null and void.

2) The same admonition not to add or subtract words is used in *Deuteronomy* 4:2, which says, "You shall not add to the word that I speak to you, neither shall you take away from it: keep the commandment of the Lord your God which I command you." If we were to apply a parallel interpretation to this verse, then anything in the Bible beyond the decrees of the Old Testament law would be considered non-canonical or not authentic Scripture—including the New Testament! Once again, all Christians would reject this conclusion in no uncertain terms. The prohibition in *Revelation* 22:18-19 against "adding," therefore, cannot mean that Christians are forbidden to look to anything outside the Bible for guidance.

2. The Bible Indicates that in Addition to the Written Word, We Are to Accept Oral Tradition.

St. Paul both commends and commands the keeping of oral tradition. In *1 Corinthians* 11:2, for instance, we read, "Now I praise you, brethren, that in all things you are mindful of me: and keep my ordinances as I have delivered them to you."[4] St. Paul is obviously commending the keeping of oral tradition here, and it should be noted in particular that he extols the believers for having done so ("I praise you . . ."). Explicit in this passage is also the fact that the integrity of this Apostolic oral tradition has clearly been maintained, just as Our Lord promised it would be, through the safeguarding of the Holy Spirit (cf. *John* 16:13).

Perhaps the clearest Biblical support for oral tradition can be found in *2 Thessalonians* 2:14(15), where Christians are actually commanded: "Therefore, brethren, stand fast; and hold the traditions which you have learned, whether by word, or by our epistle." This passage is significant in that a) it shows the existence of living traditions within the Apostolic teaching, b) it tells us unequivocally that believers are firmly grounded in the Faith by adhering to these traditions, and c) it clearly states that these traditions were both written and oral. Since the Bible distinctly states here that oral traditions—authentic and Apostolic in origin—are to be "held" as a valid component of the Deposit of Faith, by what reasoning or excuse do Protestants dismiss them? By what authority do they reject a clear-cut injunction of St. Paul?

Moreover, we must consider the text in this passage. The Greek word *krateite*, here translated "hold," means "to be strong, mighty, to prevail."[5] This language is rather emphatic, and it demonstrates the importance of maintaining these traditions. Of course one must differentiate between

Tradition (upper-case "T") that is part of divine Revelation, on the one hand, and, on the other hand, Church traditions (lower-case "t") that, although good, have developed in the Church later and are not part of the Deposit of Faith. An example of something that is part of Tradition would be infant Baptism; an example of a Church tradition would be the Church's calendar of feast days of Saints. Anything that is part of Tradition is of divine origin and hence unchangeable, while Church traditions are changeable by the Church. Sacred Tradition serves as a rule of faith by showing what the Church has believed consistently through the centuries and how it has always understood any given portion of the Bible. One of the main ways in which Tradition has been passed down to us is in the doctrine contained in the ancient texts of the liturgy, the Church's public worship.

It should be noted that Protestants accuse Catholics of promoting "unbiblical" or "novel" doctrines based on Tradition, asserting that such Tradition contains doctrines which are foreign to the Bible. However, this assertion is wholly untrue. The Catholic Church teaches that Sacred Tradition contains nothing whatsoever that is contrary to the Bible. Some Catholic thinkers would even say that there is nothing in Sacred Tradition which is not also found in Scripture, at least implicitly or in seminal form. Certainly the two are at least in perfect harmony and always support each other. For some doctrines, the Church draws more from Tradition than from Scripture for its understanding, but even those doctrines are often implied or hinted at in Sacred Scripture. For example, the following are largely based on Sacred Tradition: infant Baptism, the canon of Scripture, the perpetual virginity of the Blessed Virgin Mary, Sunday (rather than Saturday) as the Lord's Day, and the Assumption of Our Lady.

Sacred Tradition complements our understanding of the Bible and is therefore not some extraneous source of Revelation which contains doctrines that are foreign to it. Quite the contrary: Sacred Tradition serves as the Church's living memory, reminding her of what the faithful have constantly and consistently believed and how to properly understand and interpret the meaning of Biblical passages.[6] In a certain way, it is Sacred Tradition which says to the reader of the Bible, "You have been reading a very important book which contains God's revelation to man. Now let me explain to you how it has always been understood and practiced by believers from the very beginning."

3. The Bible Calls the Church and Not the Bible the "Pillar and Ground of the Truth."

It is very interesting to note that in *1 Timothy* 3:15 we see, not the Bible, but the Church—that is, the living community of believers founded upon St. Peter and the Apostles and headed by their successors—called "the pillar and ground of the truth." Of course, this passage is not meant in any way to diminish the importance of the Bible, but it *is* intending to show that Jesus Christ did establish an authoritative teaching Church which was commissioned to teach "all nations." (*Matt.* 28:19). Elsewhere this same Church received Christ's promise that the gates of Hell would not prevail against it (*Matt.* 16:18), that He would always be with it (*Matt.* 28:20), and that He would give it the Holy Spirit to teach it all truth. (*John* 16:13). To the visible head of His Church, St. Peter, Our Lord said: "And I will give to thee the keys of the kingdom of heaven. And whatsoever thou shalt bind upon earth, it shall be bound also in heaven: and, whatsoever thou shalt loose on earth, it shall be loosed also in heaven." (*Matt.* 16:19). It is plainly evident from these passages that Our Lord emphasized the authority of His Church and the role it would have in safeguarding and defining the Deposit of Faith.

It is also evident from these passages that this

same Church would be infallible, for if at any time in its history it would definitively teach error to the Church as a whole in matters of faith or morals—even temporarily—it would cease being this "pillar and ground of the truth." Since a "ground" or foundation by its very nature is meant to be a permanent support, and since the above-mentioned passages do not allow for the possibility of the Church ever definitively teaching doctrinal or moral error, the only plausible conclusion is that Our Lord was very deliberate in establishing His Church and that He was referring to its infallibility when He called it the "pillar and ground of the truth."

The Protestant, however, has a dilemma here by asserting the Bible to be the sole rule of faith for believers. In what capacity, then, is the Church the "pillar and ground of the truth" if it is not to serve as an infallible authority established by Christ? How can the Church be this "pillar and ground" if it has no tangible, practical ability to serve as an authority in the life of a Christian? The Protestant would effectively deny that the Church is the "pillar and ground of the truth" by denying that the Church has the authority to teach.

Also, Protestants understand the term "church" to mean something different from what the Catholic Church understands it to mean. Protestants see "the church" as an invisible entity, and for them it refers *collectively* to all Christian believers around the world who are united by faith in Christ, despite major variations in doctrine and denominational allegiance. Catholics, on the other hand, understand it to mean not only those true believers who are united as Christ's Mystical Body, but we simultaneously understand it to refer to a visible, historical entity as well, namely, that one—and only that one—organization which can trace its lineage in an unbroken line back to the Apostles themselves: the Catholic Church. It is *this* Church and this Church *alone* which was established by Christ and which has maintained an absolute consistency in doctrine throughout its existence, and it is therefore this Church alone which can claim to be that very "pillar and ground of the truth."

Protestantism, by comparison, has known a history of doctrinal vacillations and changes, and no two denominations completely agree—even on major doctrinal issues. Such shifting and changing could not possibly be considered a foundation or "ground of the truth." When the foundation of a structure shifts or is improperly set, that structure's very support is unreliable (cf. *Matt.* 7:26-27). Since in practice the beliefs of Protestantism have undergone change both within denominations and through the continued appearance of new denominations, these beliefs are like a foundation which shifts and moves. Such beliefs therefore cease to provide the support necessary to maintain the structure they uphold, and the integrity of that structure becomes compromised. Our Lord clearly did not intend for His followers to build their spiritual houses on such an unreliable foundation.

4. Christ Tells Us to Submit to the Authority of the Church.

In *Matthew* 18:15-18 we see Christ instructing His disciples on how to correct a fellow believer. It is extremely telling in this instance that Our Lord identifies the Church rather than Scripture as the final authority to be appealed to. He Himself says that if an offending brother "will not hear the church, let him be to thee as the heathen and publican" (*Matt.* 18:17)—that is, as an outsider who is lost. Moreover, Our Lord then solemnly re-emphasizes the Church's infallible teaching authority in verse 18 by repeating His earlier statement about the power to bind and loose (*Matt.* 16:18-19), directing it this time to the Apostles as a group[7] rather than just to Peter: "Amen I say to you, whatsoever you shall bind upon earth, shall be bound also in heaven; and whatsoever you shall loose upon earth, shall be loosed also in heaven." (*Matt.* 18:18).

Of course there are instances in the Bible where Our Lord does appeal to Scripture, but in these cases He, as one having authority, was *teaching the Scriptures*; He was not allowing the Scriptures to *teach themselves*. For example, He would respond to the Scribes and the Pharisees by using Scripture precisely because they often tried to trip Him up by using Scripture. In these instances, Our Lord often demonstrates how the Scribes and Pharisees had wrong interpretations, and hence He corrects them by *properly* interpreting Scripture.

His actions do not argue that Scripture should be *sola*, or an authority in itself and, in fact, the only Christian authority. Quite the contrary; whenever Christ refers His hearers to the Scriptures, He also provides His infallible, authoritative *interpretation* of them, demonstrating that the Scriptures do *not* interpret themselves.

The Catholic Church readily acknowledges the inerrancy and authority of Scripture. But the Catholic doctrine is that the immediate rule of faith for the Christian is the teaching authority of the Church—an authority to teach and interpret both Scripture and Tradition, as *Matt.* 18:17-18 shows.

It should also be noted that implicit (perhaps even explicit) in this passage from Matthew is the fact that the "Church" must have been a visible, tangible entity established in a hierarchical fashion. Otherwise, how would anyone have known to whom the wrongdoer should be referred? If the Protestant definition of "church" were correct, then the wrongdoer would have to "hear" each and every believer who existed, hoping that there would be unanimity among them regarding the issue at hand. The inherent absurdity of this scenario is readily apparent. The only way we can make sense of Our Lord's statement here is to acknowledge that there was a definite organization, with positions of authority readily identifiable, to which an appeal could be made and from which a decisive judgment could be had.

5. Scripture Itself States that It Is Insufficient of Itself as a Teacher, but Rather Needs an Interpreter.

The Bible says in *2 Tim.* 3:17 that the man of God is "perfect, furnished to every good work." As we noted above, this verse means only that the man of God is fully supplied with Scripture; it is not a guarantee that he automatically knows how to interpret it properly. This verse at most argues only for the *material sufficiency* of Scripture, a position which is held by some Catholic thinkers today.

"Material sufficiency" would mean that the Bible in some way contains all the truths that are necessary for the believer to know; in other words, the "materials" would thus be all present or at least implied. "Formal sufficiency," on the other hand, would mean that the Bible would not only contain all the truths that are necessary, but that it would also present those truths in a perfectly clear and complete and readily understandable fashion. In other words, these truths would be in a useable "form," and consequently there would be no need for Sacred Tradition to clarify and complete them or for an infallible teaching authority to interpret correctly or "rightly divide" God's word.

Since the Catholic Church holds that the Bible is not sufficient in itself, it naturally teaches that the Bible needs an interpreter. The reason the Catholic Church so teaches is twofold: first, because Christ established a living Church to teach with His authority. He did not simply give His disciples a Bible, whole and entire, and tell them to go out and make copies of it for mass distribution and allow people to come to whatever interpretation they may. Second, the Bible itself states that it needs an interpreter.

Regarding the second point, we read in *2 Peter* 3:16 that in St. Paul's epistles there are "certain things hard to be understood, which the unlearned and unstable wrest [distort], as they do also the other scriptures, to their own destruction."

In this one verse we note three very important things about the Bible and its interpretation: a) the Bible contains passages which are not readily understandable or clear, a fact which demonstrates the need for an authoritative and infallible teacher to make the passages clear and understandable;[8] b) it is not only possible that people *could* "wrest" or distort the meaning of Scripture, but this was, in fact, being done from the very earliest days of the Church; and c) to distort the meaning of Scripture can result in one's "destruction," a disastrous fate indeed. It is obvious from these considerations that St. Peter did not believe the Bible to be the sole rule of faith. But there is more.

In *Acts* 8:26-40 we read the account of the deacon St. Philip and the Ethiopian eunuch. In this scenario, the Holy Spirit leads Philip to approach the Ethiopian. When Philip learns that the Ethiopian is reading from the prophet *Isaias*, he asks him a very telling question: "Thinkest thou that thou understandest what thou readest?" Even more telling is the answer given by the Ethiopian: "And how can I, unless some man show me?"

Whereas this St. Philip (known as "the Evangelist") is not one of the twelve Apostles, he was nonetheless someone who was commissioned by the Apostles (cf. *Acts* 6:6) and who preached the Gospel with authority (cf. *Acts* 8:4-8). Consequently, his preaching would reflect legitimate Apostolic teaching. The point here is that the Ethiopian's statement verifies the fact that the Bible is *not* sufficient in itself as a teacher of Christian doctrine, and people who hear the Word *do* need an authority to instruct them properly so that they may understand what the Bible says. If the Bible were indeed sufficient of itself, then the eunuch would not have been ignorant of the meaning of the passage from *Isaias.*

There is also *2 Peter* 1:20, which states that "no prophecy of scripture is made by private interpretation." Here we see the Bible itself stating in no uncertain terms that its prophecies are not a matter for which the individual is to arrive at his own interpretation. It is also most telling that this verse is preceded by a section on the Apostolic witness (verses 12-18) and followed by a section on false teachers (chapter 2, verses 1-10). St. Peter is obviously contrasting genuine, Apostolic teaching with false prophets and false teachers, and he makes reference to private interpretation as the pivotal point between the two. The clear implication is that private interpretation is one pathway whereby an individual turns from authentic teaching and begins to follow erroneous teaching.

6. The First Christians Did Not Have a Complete Bible.

Biblical scholars tell us that the last book of the New Testament was not written until the end of the 1st century A.D., that is, until around the year 100 A.D.[9] This fact would leave roughly a 65-year gap between Our Lord's Ascension into Heaven and the completion of the Bible as we know it. The question that begs to be asked, therefore, is this: "Who or what served as the final, infallible authority during that time?"

If the Protestant doctrine of *Sola Scriptura* were true, then since the Church existed for a time without the entire written Word of God, there would have been situations and doctrinal issues which could not have been resolved with finality until all of the New Testament books were complete. The ship would have been left without a rudder, so to speak, at least for a time. But this goes contrary to the statements and promises that Our Lord made about His Church—particularly, "behold I am with you all days, even to the consummation of the world" (*Matt.* 28:20)—not to mention that He told His disciples: "I will not leave you orphans." (*John* 14:18).

This issue is of particular importance, as the first several decades of the Church's existence were tumultuous. Persecutions had already begun, believers were being martyred, the new Faith was struggling to grow, and some false teachings had already appeared (cf. *Galatians* 1:6-9). If the Bible were the Christian's only rule of faith, and since the Bible was not fully written—much less settled in terms of its canon—until 65 years after Christ's Ascension, how did the early Church possibly deal with doctrinal questions without an authority on how to proceed?

Now the Protestant may be tempted to offer two possible responses: 1) that the Apostles were temporarily the final authority while the New Testament was being written, and 2) that the Holy Spirit was given to the Church and that His direct guidance is what bridged the time gap between Our Lord's Ascension and the completion of the New Testament.

Regarding the first response, it is true that Jesus Christ invested the Apostles with His authority; however, the Bible nowhere indicates that this authority's active role within the Church would cease with the death of the last Apostle. Quite the contrary, the Bible record is quite clear in that a) it nowhere says that once the last Apostle dies, the *written* form of God's Word will become the final authority; and b) the Apostles clearly chose successors who, in turn, possessed the same authority to "bind and loose." This is shown in the election of Matthias as a replacement for Judas Iscariot (cf. *Acts* 1:15-26) and in St. Paul's passing on his Apostolic authority to Timothy and Titus (cf. *2 Timothy* 1:6, and *Titus* 1:5). If anything, a Protestant only gives credence to the Catholic teaching by insisting on the authority of the Apostles.

Regarding the second response—that the Holy Spirit's direct guidance bridged the time gap—the problem with such a position is that the direct guidance of the Holy Spirit Himself is an extra-Biblical (that is, "outside of the Bible") source of authority. Naturally the Bible speaks very clearly of the Holy Spirit's presence among believers and His role in teaching the disciples "all truth," but if the *direct* guidance of the Holy Spirit were, in fact, the ultimate authority during those 65 years, then the history of the Church would have known two successive ultimate authorities: first the direct guidance of the Holy Spirit, with this guidance then being replaced by the Scriptures, which would then have become *sola,* or the "only" ultimate authority. And if this situation of an extra-Biblical ultimate authority is permissible from a Protestant perspective, does this not open the door to the Catholic position, which says that the teaching authority of the Church is the direct ultimate authority—deriving her authority from Christ and her teaching from Scripture and Tradition, guided by the Holy Spirit.

The Holy Spirit was given to the Church by Jesus Christ, and it is exactly this same Spirit who protects the Church's visible head, the Pope, and the teaching authority of the Church by never permitting him or it to lapse into error. The Catholic believes that Christ indeed did give the Holy Spirit to the Church and that the Holy Spirit has always been present in the Church, teaching it all truth (*John* 16:13) and continually safeguarding its doctrinal integrity, particularly through the office of the Pope. Thus the Gospel would still have been preached—authoritatively and infallibly—even if not a single verse of the New Testament had ever been written.

7. The Church Produced the Bible and Not Vice-Versa.

The doctrine of *Sola Scriptura* overlooks—or at least grossly underemphasizes—the fact that the Church came before the Bible, and not the other way around. It was the Church, in effect, which wrote the Bible under the inspiration of Almighty God: the Israelites as the Old Testament Church (or "pre-Catholics") and the early Catholics as the New Testament Church.

In the pages of the New Testament we note that Our Lord gives a certain primacy to the teaching authority of His Church and its proclamation in His name. For instance, in *Matthew* 28:20 we see Our Lord commissioning the Apostles to go and *teach* in His name, making disciples of all nations. In *Mark* 16:15 we note that the Apostles are commanded to go and *preach* to all the world. And in *Luke* 10:16 we see that whoever *hears* the seventy-two hears Our Lord. These facts are most telling, *as nowhere do we see Our Lord commissioning His Apostles to evangelize the world by writing in*

His name. The emphasis is always on *preaching* the Gospel, not on printing and distributing it.

Thus it follows that the leadership and teaching authority of the Church are indispensable elements in the means whereby the Gospel message is to reach the ends of the earth. Since the Church produced the Scriptures, it is quite biblical, logical and reasonable to say that the Church alone has the authority to interpret properly and apply them. And if this is so, then by reason of its origin and nature, the Bible cannot serve as the *only* rule of faith for Christian believers. In other words, by producing the Scriptures, the Church does not eliminate the need for itself as teacher and interpreter of those Scriptures.

Moreover, is it not unreasonable to say that simply by putting Apostolic teaching into writing, the Church somehow made that written teaching superior to her oral teaching? Like the teaching organization Our Lord established, His Word is authoritative, but because that Word is in one *form* rather than another does not mean one form is to be subjugated to the other. Since God's *one* Revelation is *twofold* in form, to deny the authority of one form would be to deny the authority of the other form as well. The forms of God's Word are complementary, not competitive. Thus, if there is a need for the Scriptures, there is also a need for the teaching authority which produced them.

8. The Idea of the Scriptures' Authority Existing Apart from the Authority of the Teaching Church Is Utterly Foreign to the Early Church.

If you look at the writings of the Early Church Fathers, you will see references to Apostolic Succession,[10] to the bishops as guardians of the Deposit of Faith,[11] and to the primacy and the authority of Rome.[12] The collective weight of these references makes clear the fact that the early Church understood itself as having a hierarchy which was central to maintaining the integrity of the Faith. Nowhere do we see any indication that the early followers of Christ disregarded those positions of authority and considered them invalid as a rule of faith. Quite the contrary, we see in those passages that the Church, from its very inception, saw its power to teach grounded in an inseparable combination of Scripture and Apostolic Tradition—with both being authoritatively taught and interpreted by the teaching Magisterium of the Church, with the Bishop of Rome at its head.

To say that the early Church believed in the notion of "the Bible alone" would be analogous to saying that men and women today could entertain the thought that our civil laws could function without Congress to legislate them, without courts to interpret them and without police to enforce them. All we would need is a sufficient supply of legal volumes in every household so that each citizen could determine for himself how to understand and apply any given law. Such an assertion is absurd, of course, as no one could possibly expect civil laws to function in this manner. The consequence of such a state of affairs would undoubtedly be total anarchy.

How much more absurd, then, is it to contend that the Bible could function on its own and apart from the Church which wrote it? It is precisely that Church—and not just any Christian—who alone possesses the divinely given authority to interpret it correctly, as well as to legislate matters involving the conduct of its members. Were this not the case, the situation on any level—local, regional or global—would quickly devolve into spiritual anarchy, wherein each and every Christian could formulate a theological system and develop a moral code based simply upon his own private interpretation of Scripture.

Has not history actually seen precisely this result since the 16th century, when the so-called Reformation occurred? In fact, an examination of the state of affairs in Europe immediately following the genesis of the Reformation—particularly in Germany—will demonstrate that the direct result of Reformation teaching was both spiritual and social disorder.[13] Luther himself bemoaned the fact that, "Unfortunately, it is our daily experience that now under the Gospel [his] the people entertain greater and bitterer hatred and envy and are worse with their avarice and money-grabbing than before under the Papacy."[14]

9. Heresiarchs and Heretical Movements Based Their Doctrines on Scripture Interpreted Apart from Tradition and the Magisterium.

If you look at the history of the early Church, you will see that it continually struggled against heresies and those who promoted them. We also see the Church responding to those threats again and again by convening councils[15] and turning to Rome to settle disputes in matters of doctrine and discipline. For example, Pope Clement intervened in a controversy in the Church at Corinth at the end of the 1st century and put an end to a schism there. In the 2nd century, Pope Victor threatened to excommunicate a large portion of the Church in the East because of a dispute about when Easter should be celebrated. In the earlier part of the 3rd century, Pope Callistus pronounced the condemnation of the Sabellian heresy.

In the case of these heresies and/or conflicts in discipline that would arise, the people involved would defend their erroneous beliefs by their respective interpretations of Scripture, apart from Sacred Tradition and the teaching Magisterium of

the Church. A good illustration of this point is the
case of Arius, the 4th-century priest who declared
that the Son of God was a creature and was not
co-equal with the Father.

Arius and those who followed him quoted
verses from the Bible to "prove" their claims.[16]
The disputes and controversies which arose over
his teachings became so great that the first Ecumenical Council was convened in Nicaea in 325
A.D. to settle them. The Council, under the
authority of the Pope, declared Arius' teachings
to be heretical and made some decisive declarations about the person of Christ, and it did so
based on what Sacred Tradition had to say regarding the Scripture verses in question.

Here we see the teaching authority of the
Church being used as the final say in an extremely
important doctrinal matter. If there had been no
teaching authority to appeal to, then Arius' error
could have overtaken the Church. As it is, a majority of the bishops at that time fell for the Arian
heresy.[17] Even though Arius had based his arguments on the Bible and probably "compared Scripture with Scripture," the fact is that he arrived at
an heretical conclusion. It was the teaching authority of the Church—hierarchically constituted—
which stepped in and declared he was wrong.

The application is obvious. If you ask a Protestant whether or not Arius was correct in his belief
that the Son was created, he will, of course,

respond in the negative. Emphasize, then, that even though Arius presumably "compared Scripture with Scripture," he nonetheless arrived at an erroneous conclusion. If this were true for Arius, what guarantee does the Protestant have that it is not also true for *his* interpretation of a given Bible passage? The very fact that the Protestant knows Arius' interpretations were heretical implies that an objectively true or "right" interpretation exists for the Biblical passages he used. The issue, then, becomes a question of how we can know what that true interpretation is. The only possible answer is that there must be, out of necessity, an infallible authority to tell us. That infallible authority, the Catholic Church, declared Arius heretical. Had the Catholic Church not been both infallible and authoritative in its declaration, then believers would have had no reason whatsoever to reject Arius' teachings, and the whole of Christianity today might have been comprised of modern-day Arians.

It is evident, then, that using the Bible alone is not a guarantee of arriving at doctrinal truth. The above-described result is what happens when the erroneous doctrine of *Sola Scriptura* is used as a guiding principle, and the history of the Church and the numerous heresies it has had to address are undeniable testimony to this fact.

10. The Canon of the Bible Was Not Settled until the 4th Century.

One historical fact which proves extremely inconvenient for the Protestant is the fact that the canon of the Bible—the authoritative list of exactly which books are part of inspired Scripture—was not settled and fixed until the end of the 4th century. Until that time, there was much disagreement over which Biblical writings were considered inspired and Apostolic in origin. The Biblical canon varied from place to place: some lists contained books that were later defined as non-canonical, while other lists failed to include books which were later defined as canonical. For example, there were Early Christian writings which were considered by some to be inspired and Apostolic and which were actually read in Christian public worship, but which were later omitted from the New Testament canon. These include *The Shepherd of Hermas, The Epistle of Barnabas* and *The Didache*, among others.[18]

It was not until the Synod of Rome (382) and the Councils of Hippo (393) and Carthage (397) that we find a definitive list of canonical books being drawn up, and each of these Councils acknowledged the very same list of books.[19] From this point on, there is in practice no dispute about the canon of the Bible, the only exception being the so-called Protestant Reformers, who entered upon the scene in 1517, an unbelievable *11 centuries later*.

Once again, there are two fundamental questions for which one cannot provide answers that are consonant with *Sola Scriptura*: a) Who or what served as the final Christian authority up to the time that the New Testament's canon was identified? b) And if there was a final authority that the Protestant recognizes before the establishment of the canon, on what basis did that authority cease being final once the Bible's canon was established?

11. An "Extra-Biblical" Authority Identified the Canon of the Bible.

Since the Bible did not come with an inspired table of contents, the doctrine of *Sola Scriptura* creates yet another dilemma: How can one know with certainty which books belong in the Bible— specifically, in the New Testament? The unadulterated fact is that one *cannot* know unless there is an authority outside the Bible which can tell him. Moreover, this authority must, by necessity, be infallible, since the possibility of error in identifying the canon of the Bible[20] would mean that all believers run the risk of having the wrong books in their Bibles, a situation which would vitiate *Sola Scriptura*. But if there *is* such an infallible authority, then the doctrine of *Sola Scriptura* crumbles.

Another historical fact very difficult to reconcile with the doctrine of *Sola Scriptura* is that it was none other than the Catholic Church which eventually identified and ratified the canon of the Bible. The three councils mentioned above were all councils of this Church. The Catholic Church gave its final, definitive, infallible definition of the Biblical canon at the Council of Trent in 1546—naming the very same list of 73 books that had been included in the 4th century. If the Catholic Church is able, then, to render an authoritative and infallible decision concerning such an important matter as which books belong in the Bible, then upon what basis would a person question its authority on other matters of faith and morals?

Protestants should at least concede a point which Martin Luther, their religion's founder, also conceded, namely, that the Catholic Church safeguarded and identified the Bible: "We are obliged to yield many things to the Catholics—(for example), that they possess the Word of God, which we received from them; otherwise, we should have known nothing at all about it."[21]

12. The Belief that Scripture Is "Self-Authenticating" Does Not Hold Up under Examination.

Lacking a satisfactory answer to the question of how the canon of the Bible was determined, Protestants often resort to the notion that Scripture is "self-authenticating," that is, the books of the Bible witness to themselves that they are inspired of God. The major problem with such an assertion is simply that even a cursory examination of ecclesial history will demonstrate it to be utterly untrue.

For example, several books from the New Testament—*James, Jude, 2 Peter, 2 John, 3 John,* and *Revelation*—were disputed in terms of their canonical status for quite some time. In certain places they were accepted, while simultaneously in others they were rejected. Even spiritual giants like St. Athanasius (297-373), St. Jerome (c. 342-420) and St. Augustine (354-430) had drawn up lists of New Testament books which witnessed to what was generally acknowledged as inspired in their times and places, but none of these lists corresponds exactly to the New Testament canon that was eventually identified by the Catholic Church at the end of the 4th century and which is identical to the canon that Catholics have today.[22]

If Scripture were actually "self-authenticating," why was there so much disagreement and uncertainty over these various books? Why was there any disagreement at all? Why was the canon of the Bible not identified much earlier if its books were allegedly so readily discernible? The answer that one is compelled to accept in this regard is simply that the Bible is not self-authenticating at all.

Even more interesting is the fact that some books in the Bible do not identify their own authors. The idea of self-authentication—if it were true—might be more plausible if each and every Biblical author identified himself, as we could more easily examine that author's credentials, so to speak, or at least determine who it was that claimed to be speaking for God. But in this regard the Bible leaves us ignorant in a few instances.

Take St. Matthew's Gospel as one example: Nowhere does the text indicate that it was Matthew, one of the twelve Apostles, who authored it. We are therefore left with only two possibilities for determining its authorship: 1) what Tradition has to say, and 2) Biblical scholarship. In either case, the source of determination is an extra-Biblical source and would therefore fall under condemnation by the doctrine of *Sola Scriptura*.

Now the Protestant may be saying at this point that it is unnecessary to know whether or not Matthew actually wrote this Gospel, as one's salvation does not depend on knowing whether it was Matthew or someone else. But such a view presents quite a difficulty. What the Protestant is effectively saying is that while an authentic Gospel is God's Word and is the means by which a person comes to a saving knowledge of Christ, the person has no way of knowing for certain in the case of Matthew's Gospel whether it is Apostolic in origin and consequently has no way of knowing if it is genuine (i.e., God's Word) or not. And if this Gospel's authenticity is questionable, then why include it in the Bible? If its authenticity is certain, then how is this known in the absence of self-identification by Matthew? One can only conclude that the Bible is not self-authenticating.

The Protestant may wish to fall back on the Bible's own assertion that it is inspired, citing a passage like *2 Timothy* 3:16—"All scripture, inspired of God, is profitable . . ." However, a *claim* to inspiration is not in and of itself a *guarantee* of inspiration. Consider the fact that the writings of Mary Baker Eddy, the founder of the Christian Science sect, claim to be inspired. The writings of Joseph Smith, the founder of the Mormon sect, claim to be inspired. These are but two of many possible examples which demonstrate the fact that any particular writing can claim just about anything. Obviously, in order for us to know with certainty whether or not a writing is genuinely inspired, we need more than a mere claim by that writing that it is inspired. The guarantee of inspiration must come from outside that writing. In the case of the Bible, the guarantee must come from a non-Biblical source. But outside authentication is excluded by the doctrine of *Sola Scriptura*.

13. None of the Original Biblical Manuscripts Is Extant.

A sobering consideration—and one which is fatal to the doctrine of *Sola Scriptura*—is that we do not possess a single original manuscript of any book of the Bible. Now it is true that there are thousands of manuscripts extant which are *copies* of the originals—and more likely than not they are copies of copies—but this fact does not help the *Sola Scriptura* position for the simple reason that without original manuscripts, one cannot know with certainty if he actually possesses the real Bible, whole and entire.[23] The original autographs were inspired, while copies of them are not.

The Protestant may want to assert that not having original Biblical manuscripts is immaterial, as God preserved the Bible by safeguarding its duplication through the centuries.[24] However, there are two problems with this line of reasoning. The first is that by maintaining God's providence with regard to copying, a person claims something which is not written in Scripture, and therefore, by the very definition of *Sola Scriptura*, cannot serve as a rule of faith. In other words, if one cannot find passages in the Bible which patently state that God will protect the transmission of manuscripts, then the belief is not to be held. The fact of the matter is that the Bible makes no such claim.

The second problem is that if you can maintain that God safeguarded the *written* transmission of His word, then you can also rightly maintain that He safeguarded its *oral* transmission as well (recall *2 Thessalonians* 2:14(15) and the twofold form of God's one revelation). After all, the preaching of the Gospel began as an *oral* tradition (cf. *Luke* 1:1-4 and *Rom.* 10:17). It was not until later on that some of the oral tradition was committed to writing—becoming Sacred Scripture—and it was later still that these writings were declared to be inspired and authoritative. Once you can maintain that God safeguarded the oral transmission of His teaching, you have demonstrated the basis for Sacred Tradition and have already begun supporting the Catholic position.

14. The Biblical Manuscripts Contain Thousands of Variations.

It has just been noted that there are thousands of Biblical manuscripts in existence; these manuscripts contain thousands of variations in the text;

one writer estimates that there are over 200,000 variations.[25] Whereas the majority of these deal with minor concerns—such as spelling, word order and the like—there are also variations of a more important nature: a) the manuscript evidence shows that scribes sometimes modified the Biblical texts to harmonize passages, to accommodate them to historical fact, and to establish a doctrinal correctness;[26] and b) there are portions of verses (i.e., more than just a single word in question) for which there are several different manuscript readings, such as *John* 7:39, *Acts* 6:8, *Colossians* 2:2 and *1 Thessalonians* 3:2.[27] These facts leave the Protestant in the position of not knowing if he possesses what the Biblical authors originally wrote. And if this is the case, then how can a Protestant profess to base his beliefs solely on the Bible when he cannot determine with certainty the textual authenticity of the Bible?[28]

More importantly, there are several more major textual variations among New Testament manuscripts. The following two examples will illustrate the point:

First, according to the manuscripts that we have, there are four possible endings for St. Mark's Gospel: the short ending, which includes verses 1-8 of chapter 16; the longer ending, which includes verses 1-8 plus verses 9-20; the intermediate ending, which includes 2 to 3 lines of text between verse 8 and the longer ending; and the longer ending in expanded form, which includes several verses after verse 14 of the longer ending.[29] The best that can be said about these different endings is that we simply do not know for certain, from the Bible itself, where St. Mark's Gospel concluded, and, depending on which ending(s) is/are included in a Protestant's Bible, the publisher runs the risk of either adding verses to or omitting verses from the original text—thus violating the doctrine of *Sola Scriptura*, which requires "the Bible alone and in its entirety" as the basis of faith. Even if a Protestant's Bible includes all four endings with explanatory comments and/or footnotes, he still cannot be certain which of the four endings is genuine.

Second, there is manuscript evidence for alternate readings in some pivotal verses of the Bible, such as *John* 1:18, where there are two possible wordings.[30] Some (such as the King James Version) read along the lines of the Douay-Rheims: "No man hath seen God at any time: the only begotten *Son* who is in the bosom of the Father, he hath declared him." Others read along the lines of the New International Version: "No one has ever seen God, but *God* the One and Only, who is at the Father's side, has made him known." Either wording is substantiated by manuscript evidence, and you will therefore find Biblical scholars relying on their best educated judgment as to which one is "correct." A similar situation occurs at

Acts 20:28, where the manuscript evidence shows that St. Paul could be referring to either the "church of the *Lord*" (Greek *kuriou*) or the "church of *God*" (Greek *theou*).[31]

Now this point may seem trivial at first, but suppose you are trying to evangelize a cult member who denies the divinity of Jesus Christ. While *John* 1:18 and *Acts* 20:28 are clearly not the only passages to use in defense of Our Lord's divinity, you still may be unable to utilize these verses with that person, depending on which manuscript tradition your Bible follows. That would leave you marginally less able to defend a major Biblical doctrine, and the very nature of this fact becomes quite problematic from the perspective of the doctrine of *Sola Scriptura*.

15. There Are Hundreds of Bible Versions.

As mentioned in Point 14 above, there are thousands and thousands of variations in the Biblical manuscripts. This problem is compounded by the fact that history has known hundreds of Bible versions, which vary in translation as well as textual sources. The question which begs to be asked is, "Which version is the correct one?" or "Which version is closest to the original manuscripts?" One possible answer will depend on which side of the Catholic/Protestant issue you situate yourself. Another possible answer will depend upon which Bible scholars you consider to be trustworthy and reputable.

The simple fact is that some versions are clearly inferior to others. Progress in the field of Biblical research made possible by archaeological discoveries (e.g., the Dead Sea Scrolls) has vastly improved our knowledge of the ancient Biblical languages and settings. We know more today about the variables impacting upon Biblical studies than our counterparts of 100, 200 or 1,000 years ago. From this point of view, modern Bible versions may have a certain superiority to older Bible versions. On the other hand, Bibles based on the old Latin Vulgate of St. Jerome (4th century)—in English, this is the Douay-Rheims—are based on original texts which have since perished, and thus these traditional versions bypass 16 centuries of possible textual corruption.

This fact causes a considerable problem for the Protestant, because it means that modern Protestants may have in some respects a "better" or more accurate Bible than their forebears, while in other respects they may have a "poorer" or less accurate Bible—which in turn means that modern Protestants have either a "more authoritative" final authority or a "less authoritative" final authority than their predecessors. But the existence of degrees of authoritativeness begins to undermine *Sola Scriptura*, because it would mean that one Bible is not as authentic a final authority as another one. And if it is not as authentic, then the possibility of transmitting erroneous doctrine increases, and the particular Bible version then fails to function as the final authority, since it is not actually *final*.

Another point to consider is that Bible translators, as human beings, are not completely objective and impartial. Some may be likely to render a given passage in a manner which corresponds more closely with one belief system rather than with another. An example of this tendency can be seen in Protestant Bibles where the Greek word *paradoseis* occurs. Since Protestants deny the existence of Sacred Tradition, some Protestant translations of the Bible render this word as "teachings" or "customs" rather than "tradition," as the latter would tend to give more weight to the Catholic position.

Yet another consideration is the reality that some versions of the Bible are outright perversions of the Biblical texts, as in the case of the Jehovah's Witnesses' *New World Translation*. Here the "translators" render key passages in a manner which suits their erroneous doctrines.[32] Now unless there is an authority outside of the Bible to declare such translations unreliable and dangerous, by what authority could someone call them unsuited for use in teaching doctrine? If the

Protestant responds by saying that this issue can be determined on the basis of Biblical scholarship, then he is ignorant of the fact that the Jehovah's Witnesses also cite sources of Biblical scholarship in support of their translation of these passages! The issue then devolves into a game of pitting one source of scholarship against another—one human authority against another.

Ultimately, the problem can only be resolved through the intervention of an infallible teaching authority which speaks on behalf of Christ. The Catholic knows that that authority is the Roman Catholic Church and its Magisterium or teaching authority. In an exercise of this authority, Catholic Bishops grant an *Imprimatur* (meaning "Let it be printed") to be included in the opening pages of certain Bible versions and other spiritual literature to alert the reader that the book contains nothing contrary to the teachings of Christ and the Apostles.[33]

16. The Bible Was Not Available to Individual Believers until the 15th Century.

Essential to the doctrine of *Sola Scriptura* is the idea that the Holy Spirit will enlighten each believer as to the correct interpretation for a given Bible passage. This idea presupposes that each believer possesses a Bible or at least has access to a Bible. The difficulty with such a presumption is that the Bible was not able to be mass-produced and readily available to individual believers until the advent of the printing press in the 15th century.[34] Even then, it would have taken quite some time for large numbers of Bibles to be printed and disseminated to the general population.

The predicament caused by this state of affairs is that millions upon millions of Christians who lived prior to the 15th century would have been left without a final authority, left to flounder spiritually, unless by chance they had access to a hand-copied Bible. Even a mere human understanding of such circumstances would make God out to be quite cruel, as He would have revealed the fullness of His Word to humanity in Christ, knowing that the means by which such information could be made readily available would not exist for another 15 centuries.

On the other hand, we know that God is not cruel at all, but in fact has infinite love for us. It is for this reason that He did not leave us in darkness. He sent us His Son to teach us the way we should believe and act, and this Son established a Church to promote those teachings through preaching to both the learned and the illiterate. "Faith then cometh by hearing; and hearing by the word of Christ." (*Rom.* 10:17). Christ also gave to His Church His guarantee that He would always be with it, never allowing it to fall into error. God, therefore, did not abandon His people and make them rely upon the invention of the printing press to be the means whereby they would come to a saving knowledge of His Son. Instead, He gave us a divinely established, infallible teacher, the Catholic Church, to provide us with the means to be informed of the Good News of the Gospel— and to be informed correctly.

17. The Doctrine of *Sola Scriptura* Did Not Exist Prior to the 14th Century.

As difficult a reality as it may be for some to face, this foundational doctrine of Protestantism did not originate until the 14th century and did not become widespread until the 16th century—a far, far cry time-wise from the teachings of Jesus Christ and His Apostles. This simple fact is conveniently overlooked or ignored by Protestants, but it can stand alone as sufficient reason to discard the doctrine of *Sola Scriptura*. The truth is that the doctrine of *Sola Scriptura* did not exist before John Wycliffe (forerunner of Protestantism) in the 14th century and did not become widespread until Martin Luther came along in the 16th century and began setting up his own "traditions of men" in place of authentic Christian teaching. The doctrine, therefore, not only lacks the historical continuity which marks legitimate Apostolic teaching, but it actually represents an abrupt change, a radical break with the Christian past.

Protestants will assert that the Bible itself teaches *Sola Scriptura* and therefore that the doctrine had its roots back with Jesus Christ. However, as we have seen above, the Bible teaches no such thing. The claim that the Bible teaches this doctrine is nothing more than a repeated effort to retroject this belief back into the pages of Scripture. The examination of historical continuity (or lack thereof) provides an indication whether or not a particular belief originated with Jesus Christ and the Apostles or whether it appeared somewhere much later in time. The fact is that the historical record is utterly silent on the doctrine of *Sola Scriptura* prior to the 14th century.

18. The Doctrine of *Sola Scriptura* Produces Bad Fruit, Namely, Division and Disunity.

If the doctrine of *Sola Scriptura* were true, then it should be expected that Protestants would all be in agreement in terms of doctrine, as the Bible could not simultaneously teach contradictory beliefs. And yet the reality is that there are literally thousands[35] of Protestant sects and denominations, each of which claims to have the Bible as its only guide, each of which claims to be preaching the truth, yet each of which teaches something different from the others. Protestants claim that they differ only in non-essential or peripheral matters, but the fact is that they cannot even agree on major doctrinal issues such as the Eucharist, salvation, and justification—to name a few.

For instance, most Protestant denominations teach that Jesus Christ is only symbolically present in the Eucharist, while others (such as Lutherans and Episcopalians) believe that He is literally present, at least to some extent. Some denominations teach that once you are "saved" you can never lose your salvation, while others believe it is possible for a true Christian to sin gravely and cease being "saved." And some denominations teach that justification involves the Christian's being merely *declared* righteous, while others teach that the Christian must also grow in holiness and actually *become* righteous.

Our Lord categorically never intended for His followers to be as fragmented, disunited and chaotic as the history of Protestantism has been since its very inception.[36] Quite the contrary, He prayed for His followers: "That they all may be one, as thou, Father, in me, and I in thee; that they also may be one in us." (*John* 17:21). And St. Paul exhorts Christians to doctrinal unity with the words, "One body and one Spirit . . . One Lord, one faith, one baptism." (*Eph.* 4:4-5). How, then, can the thousands of Protestant denominations and sects all claim to be the "true Church" when their very existence refutes this claim? How can such heterodoxy and contradiction in doctrine be the unity for which Our Lord prayed?

In this regard, the reader should be reminded of Christ's own words: "For by the fruit the tree is known." (*Matt.* 12:33). By this standard, the historical testimony afforded by Protestantism demonstrates that the tree of *Sola Scriptura* is producing bad fruit.

19. The Doctrine of *Sola Scriptura* Does Not Allow for a Final, Definitive Interpretation of any given Passage of Scripture.

As we have seen above, the doctrine of *Sola Scriptura* maintains that the individual believer needs only the Bible as a rule of faith and that he can obtain a true interpretation of a given Scripture passage simply by comparing it with what the rest of the Bible teaches. In practice, however, this approach creates more problems than it solves, and it ultimately prevents the believer from knowing *definitively and with certainty* how any given passage from the Bible should be interpreted.

The Protestant, in reality, interprets the Bible

from a standpoint of subjective opinion rather than objective truth. For example, say Protestant person A studies a Scripture passage and concludes interpretation X. Protestant B studies the identical passage and concludes interpretation Y. Lastly, Protestant C studies the same passage and concludes interpretation Z.[37] Interpretations X and Y and Z are mutually contradictory. Yet each of these people, from the Protestant perspective, can consider his or her interpretation to be "correct" because each one has "compared Scripture with Scripture."

Now there are only two possible determinations for these three Protestants: a) each of them is incorrect in his interpretation, or b) only one of them is correct—since three contradictory interpretations cannot simultaneously be true.[38] The problem here is that, without the existence of an infallible authority to tell the three Protestants which of their respective interpretations is correct (i.e., objectively true), there is no way for each of them to know with certainty and definitively if his particular interpretation is the correct one. Each Protestant is ultimately left to an individual interpretation based on mere personal opinion—study and research into the matter notwithstanding. Each Protestant thus becomes his own final authority—or, if you will, his own "pope."

Protestantism in practice bears out this fact. Since the Bible alone is not sufficient as a rule of faith (if it were, our three Protestants would be in complete accord in their interpretations), every believer and denomination within Protestantism must necessarily arrive at his/her/its own interpretation of the Bible. Consequently, if there are many possible interpretations of Scripture, by definition there is no ultimate interpretation. And if *there is no ultimate interpretation*, then a person cannot know whether or not his own interpretation is objectively true.

A good comparison would be the moral law. If each person relied on his own opinion to determine what was right or wrong, we would have nothing more than moral relativism, and each person could rightly assert his own set of standards. However, since God has clearly defined moral absolutes for us (in addition to those we can know by reason from the natural law), we can assess any given action and determine how morally good or bad it is. This would be impossible without moral absolutes.

Of course any given denomination within Protestantism would probably maintain that its particular interpretations are the correct ones—at least in practice, if not formally. If it did not, its adherents would be changing denominations! However, if any given denomination claims that its interpretations are correct above those of the other denominations, it has effectively set itself up as a final authority. The problem here is that such an act violates *Sola Scriptura*, setting up an authority outside Scripture.

On the other hand, if any given denomination would grant that its interpretations are no more correct than those of other denominations, then we are back to the original dilemma of never knowing which interpretation is correct and thus never having the definitive truth. But Our Lord said, "I am the way, and the truth, and the life." (*John* 14:6). The predicament here is that each and every denomination within Protestantism makes the same claim—either effectively or formally—regarding its interpretations being "correct." What we are left with are thousands of different denominations, each claiming to have the Scriptural "truth," yet none of which is capable of providing an objective determination regarding that "truth." The result is an inability to obtain a definitive, authoritative and final interpretation of any given Scripture passage. In other words, the Protestant can never say that "the buck stops here" with regard to any given interpretation for any given passage of the Bible.

20. The Protestant Bible Is Missing 7 Entire Books.

Much to their chagrin, Protestants are actually guilty of violating their own doctrine. The doctrine of *Sola Scriptura* prohibits anyone from adding to or deleting from the Bible, but Protestants have, in fact, deleted seven entire books from the Old Testament, as well as portions of two others. The books in question, which are wrongly termed "the Apocrypha" ("not authentic") by Protestants, are called the "deuterocanonical" ("second canon") books by Catholics; they are *Tobias* (*Tobit*), *Judith, 1* and *2 Machabees, Wisdom, Ecclesiasticus* (or *Sirach*), and *Baruch*. Portions of *Daniel* and *Esther* are also missing.

In defense of their deficient Old Testament canon, Protestants invariably present one or more of the following arguments: 1) the shorter, Pharisaic (or Palestinian) canon[39] of the Old Testament was accepted by Christ and His Apostles, as they never quoted from the deuterocanonical books; 2) the Old Testament was closed by the time of Christ, and it was the shorter canon; 3) the Jews themselves accepted the shorter, Pharisaic canon at the council of Jamnia (or Javneh) in 90 A.D.; and 4) the deuterocanonical books contain unscriptural material.

Each of these arguments is wholly flawed.

1) Regarding the claim that Christ and His Apostles accepted the shorter, Pharisaic canon, an examination of the New Testament's quotation of the Old Testament will demonstrate its fallacy. The New Testament quotes the Old Testament about 350 times, and in approximately 300 of those

instances (86%), the quotation is taken from the Septuagint, a Greek translation of the Old Testament in widespread use at the time of Christ. The Septuagint contained the deuterocanonical books. It is therefore unreasonable and presumptuous to say that Christ and His Apostles accepted the shorter Old Testament canon, as the clear majority of the time they used an Old Testament version which did contain the seven books in question.

Or, take the case of St. Paul, whose missionary journeys and letters were directed to Hellenistic regions outside of Palestine. It has been noted, for example, that his sermon at Antioch in Pisidia "presupposed a thorough acquaintance among his hearers with the Septuagint" and that once a Christian community had been founded, the content of his letters to its members "breathed the Septuagint."[40] Obviously, St. Paul was supporting the longer canon of the Old Testament by his routine appeal to the Septuagint.

Moreover, it is erroneous to say either that the deuterocanonical books were never quoted by Christ[41] and His Apostles or that such citation is a prerequisite for a book's inclusion in the Biblical canon. According to one list, the deuterocanonical books are cited or alluded to in the New Testament not less than 150 times![42] In addition, there are Old Testament books, such as *Ecclesiastes*, *Esther* and *Abdias* (*Obadiah*), which are not quoted by Christ or the Apostles, but which are nonetheless included in the Old Testament canon (both Catholic and Protestant). Obviously, then, citation by Christ or the Apostles does not single-handedly determine canonicity.

2) Regarding the claim that Christ and the Apostles worked with a closed Old Testament canon—which Protestants maintain was the shorter canon—the historical evidence undermines the allegation. First, there was no entity known as *the* Palestinian canon, for there were actually three canons in use in Palestine at that time,[43] in addition to the Septuagint canon. And second, the evidence demonstrates that "Judaism in the last two centuries B.C. and in the first century A.D. was by no means uniform in its understanding of which of its writings were considered sacred. There were many views both inside and outside of Israel in the first centuries B.C. and A.D. on which writings were deemed sacred."[44]

3) Using the Council of Jamnia in support of a shorter canon is manifestly problematic for the following reasons: a) The decisions of a Jewish council which was held more than 50 years after the Resurrection of Christ are in no way binding on the Christian community, just as the ritual laws of Judaism (e.g., the prohibition against eating pork) are not binding on Christians. b) It is questionable whether or not the council made final decisions about the Old Testament canon of Scripture, since "the list of books acknowledged to

'defile the hands' continued to vary within Judaism itself up through the 4th century A.D."[45] c) The council was, to some extent, a polemic directed specifically against the "sect" of Christianity, and its tone, therefore, was inherently opposed to Christianity. These Jews most likely accepted the shorter Pharisaic canon precisely because the early Christians accepted the longer Septuagint canon. d) The decisions of this council represented the judgment of just one branch of Pharasaic Judaism within Palestine and not of Judaism as a whole.

4) Lastly, for Protestants to aver that the deuterocanonical books contain unscriptural material is decidedly a case of unwarranted dogmatism. This conclusion was reached simply because the so-called Reformers, who were clearly antagonistic toward the Catholic Church, approached the Bible with an *a priori* notion that it teaches "Reformed" (Protestant) doctrine. They discarded the deuterocanonical books because in certain instances these books contain decidedly Catholic doctrine, as in the case of *2 Machabees* 12:42-46, which clearly supports the doctrine of prayers for the dead and hence of Purgatory: "It is therefore a holy and wholesome thought to pray for the dead, that they may be loosed from sins." (*2 Mach.* 12:46). Luther, in fact, wanted to discard also the New Testament books of *Revelation* and *James*, the latter of which he termed an "epistle

of straw" and which he felt had "nothing evangelical about it"⁴⁶—no doubt because it clearly
states that we are saved by faith *and* works (cf.
James 2:14-26), in contrast to Luther's erroneous
"faith alone" doctrine. Luther was ultimately per-
suaded by his friends to retain these books.

In addition to the above is the fact of historical testimony and continuity regarding the canon
of the Bible. While we have seen that there were
disputes regarding the Biblical canon, two considerations are nonetheless true: 1) the deuterocanonical books were certainly used by Christians
from the 1st century onward, beginning with Our
Lord and His disciples, and 2) once the issue of
the canon was settled in the 4th century, we see
no change in Christian practice regarding the
canon from that point onward. In practice, the
only challenge to and disregard of these two real-
ities occurs when the so-called Reformers arrive
on the scene *in the 16th century* and decide that
they can simply trash an 11-centuries-long continuity regarding the canon's formal existence and
a nearly 15-centuries-long continuity regarding its
practical existence.

The fact that *any* individual would come along
and single-handedly alter such a continuity
regarding so central an issue as which books comprise the Bible should give the sincere follower of
Christ *serious pause*. Such a follower is compelled to ask, "By whose authority does this indi-

vidual make such a major change?" Both history and Luther's own writings show that Luther's actions were based on nothing but his own personal say-so. Surely such an "authority" falls *grossly* short of that which is needed for the canonical change he espoused, especially considering that the process of identifying the Bible's canon was guided by the Holy Spirit, took centuries, and involved some of the greatest minds in Christianity as well as several Church Councils. More disturbing still is the fact that the other so-called Reformers—and Protestants ever since—have followed suit by accepting Luther's changed canon, yet all the while they claim to honor the Bible and insist that nothing can be added to or deleted from it.

21. The Doctrine of *Sola Scriptura* Had its Source in Luther's Own Emotional Problems.

If anything at all can be said with certainty about Martin Luther, it is that he was deeply and chronically troubled by a combination of doubts and despair about his salvation and a sense of utter impotence in the face of temptation and sin. Luther himself notes, "My spirit was completely broken and I was always in a state of melancholy; for, do what I would, my 'righteousness' and my 'good works' brought me no help or consolation."[47]

In light of this reality, one must assess Luther's psychological and emotional frame of mind in terms of their impact on the origins of his *Sola Scriptura* doctrine. Even a cursory examination will demonstrate that this doctrine was born out of Luther's need to be free from the guilt feelings, despair and temptation which "tortured" him.

Considering that Luther himself admits to an obsessive concern with his own sinfulness, as well as an inability to resist temptation, it seems reasonable to conclude that he suffered from scrupulosity, and even Lutheran scholars will admit to this.[48] Scrupulosity means that a person is overly anxious about having committed sins when there is no real basis for such anxiety, and a scrupulous person is one who often exaggerates the severity of his perceived sinfulness, with a corresponding lack of trust in God. It is also relevant to note that scrupulosity "often seems to be based on some psychological dysfunction in the person."[49]

In other words, Luther probably never had a moment of emotional or psychological peace, since the voice of "conscience" always pricked him about some matter, real or imagined. It would be quite natural for someone so plagued to seek refuge from that voice, and for Luther that refuge was found in the doctrine of *Sola Fide*, or salvation by "faith alone."

But since the avoidance of sin as well as the performance of good works are necessary components to our salvation, and since these facts were steadfastly taught and defended by the Catholic Church, Luther found himself diametrically opposed to the teaching authority of the Church. Because the Church asserted the necessity of doing exactly what he felt incapable of doing, Luther made a drastic decision—one which "solved" his scrupulosity problem: he rejected the teaching authority of the Church, embodied in the Magisterium with the Pope at its head, and claimed that such was contrary to the Bible. In other words, by claiming *Sola Scriptura* to be true Christian doctrine, Luther dismissed that authority which compelled him to recognize that his own spirituality was dysfunctional.

Summary

For all these reasons, then, it is evident that the Protestant doctrine of *Sola Scriptura* is an utterly unbiblical, man-made, erroneous belief which must be wholly rejected. Those who are genuine Christian believers and who have a commitment to the truths that Jesus Christ taught—even if these contradict one's current religious system— should be compelled by the evidence to see the inherent flaws in this doctrine, flaws which are clearly obvious from Scripture, logic and history.

The fullness of religious truth, unmixed with error, is found only in the Catholic Church, the very Church which Jesus Christ Himself established. According to the teaching of this Church, founded by Christ, *Sola Scriptura* is a distorted, truncated view of Christian authority. Rather, the true *rule of faith* for the followers of Christ is this:

The immediate or direct *rule of faith* is the teaching of the Church; the Church in turn takes her teaching from Divine Revelation—both the written Word, called Sacred Scripture, and the oral or unwritten Word, known as "Tradition," which together form the remote or indirect *rule of faith.*

Scripture and Tradition are the inspired *sources* of Christian doctrine, while the Church—a historical and visible entity dating back to St. Peter and the Apostles in an uninterrupted succession—is the infallible *teacher* and *interpreter* of Christian doctrine. It is only by accepting this *complete* Christian rule of faith that followers of Christ can know they are adhering to *all* the things that He commanded His Apostles to teach (cf. *Matt.* 28:20). It is only by accepting this *complete* Christian rule of faith that the followers of Christ are assured of possessing the whole truth which Christ taught, and nothing but that truth.

NOTES

Note: Among the references here cited are a few Protestant authors; their works are not cited as "recommended reading," but they show that the points made in the present work are valid even by Protestant standards.

1. The Protestant Reformation was not a reform in the true sense of the word, but rather it was a revolution—an upheaval of the legitimate, established religious and civil order of the day.
2. W. E. Vine [Protestant author], *Vine's Expository Dictionary of New Testament Words* (McLean, VA: MacDonald Publishing House, n.d.), p. 387. Cf. St. Alphonsus Liguori, *An Exposition and Defense of all the Points of Faith Discussed and Defined by the Sacred Council of Trent; along with a Refutation of the Errors of the Pretended Reformers, etc.* (Dublin: James Duffy, 1846), p. 50.
3. While all the books of the New Testament are considered to have been written by the time St. John finished *The Apocalypse (Revelation)*, they were not formally identified as "the Bible" until much later on.
4. The word translated as "ordinances" is also translated "teachings" or "traditions"; for example, the New International Version gives "teachings," with a footnote: "Or *traditions*."
5. Vine, *op. cit.*, p. 564.
6. One example of this interpretive memory involves *Revelation* 12. The Early Church Fathers understood the "woman clothed with the sun" to be a reference to the Assumption of the Blessed Virgin Mary. For someone to assert that this doctrine did not exist until 1950 (the year Pope Pius XII formally defined the doctrine) represents ignorance of ecclesial history. Essentially, the belief was held from the beginning, but it was not formally *defined* until the 20th century. Bear in mind that the Church often did not have a

need to define a doctrine formally until it was formally challenged by someone (usually a heretic). Such occasions gave rise to the need officially to define the "parameters" of the doctrine in question.

7. Catholic teaching states that "'the body of bishops,'" the successors of the Apostles, also teach infallibly when they, in union with the Pope, "'exercise the supreme Magisterium,' above all in an Ecumenical Council." (Cf. *Catechism of the Catholic Church,* #891). Also, "binding and loosing" is Rabbinical terminology, and it refers to the power to pronounce authoritative interpretations and teachings. Christ clearly intended, then, for His Apostles, under the leadership of St. Peter (for St. Peter alone received the power of the keys), to possess the authority to render these authoritative interpretations and teachings.

8. The assertion by Protestants that the Bible is its own interpreter is nothing more than an exercise in futility. They claim that a person can correctly interpret any given Scripture by comparing it with what the rest of the Bible teaches. The problem with this line of reasoning can be readily demonstrated. Ask ten people to give their respective interpretations of a given Scripture passage, and you could get as many as ten different explanations. If the Bible were able to interpret itself, as Protestants claim, why do you not always obtain ten identical interpretations, even if you allow these people an ample amount of time to conduct study and research? And if this diversity of interpretation is true for a mere ten people, image the results when you multiply that number by one hundred, or one thousand, or one million. History has already seen such a result, and its name is Protestantism.

9. There are some Biblical scholars who maintain that *2 Peter* was actually the last New Testament book written, dating it sometime in the earlier part of the

2nd century. Since there is not a consensus among scholars that this date is accurate, it is sufficient for our purposes here to accept the generally held view that all of the New Testament books were complete with the composition of *Revelation*.

10. See, for instance: Irenaeus' *Against Heresies*, Book 3, Chapter 3; Tertullian's *Prescription against Heretics*, Chapter 32; and Origen's *First Principles*, Book 1, Preface.

11. See, for instance: Ignatius' *Letter to the Smyrnaeans*, Chapters 8-9; Ignatius' *Letter to the Philadelphians*, Introduction and Chapters 1-4; and Ignatius' *Letter to the Magnesians*, Chapter 7.

12. See, for instance: *1 Clement,* Chapters 1, 56, 58, 59; Ignatius' *Letter to the Romans,* introduction and Chapter 3; Irenaeus' *Against Heresies,* Book 3, Chapter 3, no. 2; Tertullian's *Prescription against Heretics,* Chapter 22; and Eusebius' *Ecclesiastical History,* Book 5, Chapter 24, no. 9.

13. See Msgr. Patrick F. O'Hare, LL.D., *The Facts about Luther* (Cincinnati: Pustet, 1916; Rockford, IL: TAN, 1987), pp. 215-255.

14. Walch, XIII, 2195, as quoted in *The Facts About Luther,* p. 15; brackets in original.

15. Bear in mind that the decrees of an Ecumenical Council had no binding force unless they were ratified by the Pope.

16. Two favorite verses for Arians of all ages to cite in support of their beliefs are *Proverbs* 8:22 and *John* 14:28.

17. See John Henry Newman, *The Arians of the Fourth Century.*

18. Henry G. Graham, *Where We Got the Bible: Our Debt to the Catholic Church* (St. Louis: B. Herder, 1911; Rockford, IL: TAN , 1977, 17th printing), pp. 34-35.

19. This list is the same as the list given in the Church's final, definitive, explicit, infallible declaration as to

which books are to be included in the Bible, which was made by the Council of Trent, Session IV, in 1546. Earlier lists of canonical books were the list in the "Decretal of Gelasius," which was issued by authority of Pope Damasus in 382, and the canon of Pope St. Innocent I, which was sent to a Frankish bishop in 405. Neither document was intended to be an infallible statement binding the whole Church, but both documents include the same 73 books as the list of Trent some 11 centuries later. (*The Catholic Encyclopedia* [New York: The Encyclopedia Press, 1913], Vol. 3, p. 272.)

20. The reader must note that the Catholic Church does not claim that by identifying the books of the Bible it *rendered* them canonical. God alone is the author of canonicity. The Catholic Church instead claims that it and it alone has the authority and responsibility of infallibly *pointing out* which books comprise the Biblical canon already authored by God.

21. *Commentary on John*, chapter 16, as cited in Paul Stenhouse's *Catholic Answers to "Bible" Christians* (Kensington: Chevalier Press, 1993), p. 31.

22. Graham, *op. cit.,* p. 31.

23. The earliest copies of the Bible, Codex Vaticanus and Codex Sinaiticus, both date from the 4th century A.D., and neither one contains the entire Bible, as parts of the manuscripts have been lost or destroyed. The vast majority of the manuscripts that exist are only portions of the Bible.

24. The irony here is that it was due to the tireless efforts of Catholic monks working laboriously in their monasteries that the written word of God survived down through the centuries. The claim that the Catholic Church did everything in its power to suppress the Bible is a most pernicious falsehood, and it can readily be refuted by even the most cursory exam-

ination of and research into Church history. Quite the contrary, the Catholic Church, in its unique role as guardian of the Deposit of Faith, protected the Bible's integrity from spurious and faulty translations, and it was these spurious and faulty copies of the Bible which it burned or destroyed to prevent false gospels from being circulated.

25. Raymond F. Collins, *Introduction to the New Testament* (Garden City, NY: Doubleday & Company, Inc., 1983), p. 77.

26. *Ibid.*, pp. 100-102.

27. Bruce M. Metzger [Protestant author], *The Text of the New Testament: Its Transmission, Corruption, and Restoration* (Oxford University Press, 1992), pp. 221-225, 234-242.

28. It has been maintained by Protestants that in all the variations in Biblical manuscripts, not one touches upon a major doctrine. Even though this assertion is untrue, it does not alter the fact that the Protestant is here admitting, at least obliquely, that it is permissible to accept something which is less than or different from the "real" Bible. And if this is true, then the Protestant himself has begun to undermine *Sola Scriptura*.

29. Metzger, *op. cit.*, pp. 226-228.

30. Collins, *op. cit.*, p. 102.

31. Metzger, *op. cit.*, p. 234.

32. Of the numerous examples which could be cited, space considerations confine us to just a few to illustrate the point. In *John* 1:1, the NWT reads, ". . . and the Word was a god" rather than "and the Word was God," because Witnesses deny the divinity of Jesus Christ. In *Colossians* 1:15-20, the NWT inserts the word "other" into the text four times because Witnesses believe that Jesus Christ Himself was created. In *Matthew* 26:26 the NWT reads ". . . this means my body . . ." instead of "This is my body," because Wit-

nesses deny the Real Presence of Christ in the Eucharist.

33. Moreover, the old Latin Vulgate version of the Bible received a very particular approval by the Church at the Council of Trent among all the Latin editions of the Scriptures then in circulation. The Council of Trent declared: "Moreover, the same Holy Council [of Trent] . . . ordains and declares that the old Latin Vulgate Edition, which, in use for so many hundred years, has been approved by the Church, be in public lectures, disputations, sermons and expositions held as authentic, and that no one dare or presume under any pretext whatsoever to reject it." (Fourth Session, April 8, 1546). Hence, as Pope Pius XII stated in his 1943 encyclical letter *Divino Afflante Spiritu* ("On the Promotion of Biblical Studies"), the Vulgate, "when interpreted in the sense in which the Church has always understood it," is "free from any error whatsoever in matters of faith and morals."

In 1907 Pope St. Pius X (1903-1914) initiated a revision of the Vulgate to achieve even greater textual accuracy. After his death, this huge project was carried on by others. In 1979 John Paul II promulgated a "New Vulgate" as "*Editio typica*" or "normative edition."

34. It should be noted that the inventor of the printing press—Johannes Gutenberg—was Catholic, and that the first book he printed was the Bible (*circa* 1455). It should also be noted that the first printed Bible contained 73 books, the exact same number as today's Catholic Bible. Protestants deleted 7 books from the Old Testament after the Bible had already begun being printed.

35. By some estimates there are approximately 25,000 different Protestant denominations and sects. In the approximately 500 years since Protestantism's origin with Martin Luther (usually dated at 1517), this num-

ber translates into an average of one new Protestant denomination or sect developing *every week*! Even if you take a conservative estimate of 10,000 denominations and sects, you still have a new one developing every 2½ weeks.

36. Even the original "Reformers"—Martin Luther, John Calvin and Ulrich Zwingli—did not agree on doctrinal matters and labeled each other's teachings heretical.

37. The quantity of three is used here for illustrative purposes only. The actual historical quantities (i.e., the number of variant interpretations for various passages) are far larger.

38. It is not denied here that a given passage from Scripture can have different levels of interpretation or that it may have different levels of meaning in terms of its application in the life of a believer. It *is*, however, denied here that a given passage can have more than one theological or doctrinal meaning in the face of opposing interpretations. For example, if two people assert, respectively, "X" and "not-X" for a given interpretation, they cannot both be correct. Take the doctrine of the Holy Eucharist, for instance. If the first person says that the bread and wine at Mass actually *become* the Body and Blood of Jesus Christ and the second person says that they do not, it is impossible for both views to be objectively true.

39. The Pharisaic canon, which was used by Jews in Palestine, did not contain the deuterocanonical books. The Septuagint or Alexandrian canon, which was used largely by Jews living in the Dispersion (i.e., Hellenistic regions outside of Palestine), did contain the deuterocanonical books.

40. W. H. C. Frend [Protestant author], *The Rise of Christianity* (Philadelphia, PA: Fortress Press, 1984), pp. 99-100.

41. For some examples, compare the following passages:

Matt. 6:14-15 with *Ecclesiasticus (Sirach)* 28:2; *Matt.* 6:7 with *Ecclesiasticus (Sirach)* 7:15(14); *Matt.* 7:12 with *Tobit (Tobias)* 4:16(15); *Luke* 12:18-20 with *Sirach* 11:19 (*Ecclus.* 11:19-20); *Acts* 10:34 with *Ecclus.* 35:15 (*Sirach* 35:12); *Acts* 10:26 with *Wisdom* 7:1; and *Matt.* 8:11 with *Baruch* 4:37.

42. Lee Martin McDonald [Protestant author], *The Formation of the Christian Biblical Canon*, Appendix A (Nashville, TN: The Parthenon Press, 1988). (Listing entitled "New Testament Citations and Allusions to Apocryphal and Pseudepigraphal Writings," adapted from *The Text of the New Testament*, by Kurt Aland and Barbara Aland, two well-known Biblical scholars.)

43. They include a) the Qumran canon, which we know of from the Dead Sea Scrolls, b) the Pharisaic canon, and c) the Sadducees/Samaritan canon, which included only the Torah (the first five books of the Old Testament).

44. McDonald, *op. cit.,* p. 53.

45. *Ibid.*, p. 60.

46. Hartmann Grisar, S.J., *Martin Luther: His Life and Work* (B. Herder, 1930; Westminster, MD: The Newman Press, 1961), p. 426.

47. Jansen, Vol. III, p. 84, as quoted in O'Hare, *op. cit.*, p. 51.

48. Cf. Fr. William Most, "Are We Saved by Faith Alone?", cassette tape from Catholic Answers, P.O. Box 17490, San Diego, CA 92177.

49. Fr. Peter Stravinskas, ed., *Catholic Encyclopedia* (Huntington, Indiana: Our Sunday Visitor, Inc., 1991), p. 873.